Gateway to God

'Modern Spirituality' series

Gateway to God

DAILY READINGS WITH MICHAEL RAMSEY

Introduced and edited by
Lorna Kendall

Darton, Longman and Todd
London

First published in 1988 by
Darton, Longman and Todd Ltd
89 Lillie Road, London SW6 1UD

© 1988 Michael Ramsey

Introduction and arrangement
© 1988 Lorna Kendall

Extracts from
The Future of the Christian Church
© 1970 Morehouse-Barlow Co. Inc.

ISBN 0 232 51774 6

British Library Cataloguing in Publication Data

Ramsey, Michael
  Gateway to God.
  1. Christian life—Daily readings
  I. Title   II. Kendall, Lorna   III. Series
  242'.2

ISBN 0–232–51774–6

Phototypeset by Input Typesetting Ltd
London SW19 8DR
Printed and bound in Great Britain by
Anchor Brendon Ltd, Tiptree, Essex

Contents

Acknowledgements

We are grateful to the following for permission to quote copyright material: Anglican and Eastern Churches Association, from *Constantinople 381*; Collins Fount, from *Be Still and Know*; Longman Group, from *The Glory of God and the Transfiguration of Christ* and *The Gospel and the Catholic Church*; Morehouse-Barlow, from *The Future of the Christian Church* (with Archbishop Suenens); A. R. Mowbray & Co. Ltd, from *The Meaning of Prayer*; SCM Press Ltd, from *God, Christ and the World*; SPCK, from *Canterbury Pilgrim*, *The Christian Priest Today*, *Durham Essays and Addresses*, *Freedom, Faith and the Future*, *Holy Spirit*, *Lent with St John*.

Introduction

Arthur Michael Ramsey was born in Cambridge on 14 November 1904, where his father, Arthur Stanley Ramsey, was a Mathematics don in the University and, later, President of Magdalene College. Michael Ramsey's childhood was spent alongside his outstandingly brilliant elder brother, who was to die in early manhood, and his two younger sisters. He was educated at Repton, where another future Archbishop of Canterbury, Geoffrey Fisher, was the Headmaster. In a different school from his brother, Michael Ramsey's academic excellence soon manifested itself, as did his outstanding ability in the school's Debating Society. Michael Ramsey's father was a Congregationalist and it was at Repton that the young Michael presented himself for Confirmation in the Church of England.

From Repton he went on to his father's college, Magdalene College, Cambridge. There, in his first term, he won the Latin Verse Prize. His remarkable versatility and force as a debater won him a place in a four-man team which toured the United States in the summer vacation of 1925, and the distinction of becoming the President of the Cambridge Union in 1926. His interests and abilities suggested that he would have had a brilliant career in law or politics or government but, with the dawning of a strong sense of vocation, he changed course and, after taking a First in the Theological Tripos, in 1927 he proceeded to

Cuddesdon Theological College to prepare for Ordination.

The tragic death in a motor accident of Michael Ramsey's mother while he was at Cuddesdon, and the unexpected death from illness three years later of his elder brother, left indelible scars on him. These personal sorrows no doubt played their part in deepening the compassion and pastoral concern of the young priest, twin ingredients both of his spiritual perception and his daily life. From 1928 to 1940 he was gaining experience in parochial work and theological teaching in a down-town parish in Liverpool; as sub-warden of Lincoln Theological College, where, at the age of thirty-two, he wrote *The Gospel and the Catholic Church*, a book which has proved to be one of the greatest theological works of the twentieth century; and as vicar of St Benet's, Cambridge.

The war was in full swing and Michael Ramsey would most likely have been called up as an army chaplain had he not, despite his youth, been appointed Canon of Durham Cathedral and Professor of Divinity in the University, where he spent ten happy years and exerted great leadership in reshaping the Theology Faculty with a team of distinguished colleagues. It was while he held the Van Mildert Chair that the young Professor Ramsey wrote two of his most perceptive and penetrating books, *The Glory of God and the Transfiguration of Christ* and *The Resurrection of Christ*. To read the former is not only to discover biblical exegesis at its best but also to stand with Moses and Elijah on the Mount of the Transfiguration; to read the latter is not only to confront the probing questions of twentieth-century critical study but also to apprehend, in the light of the Easter faith, that 'man, nature and history have their solution not within themselves but within a divine kingdom which transcends them'.

It was soon after coming to Durham that he married his wife, Joan, and there can be no doubt that the stability and happiness of their marriage have contributed enormously to the unity and authenticity of Michael Ramsey's Christian witness. Their delightful sense of fun and often irrepressible laughter, together with their warm hospitality and joyous companionship, have brought many blessings of friendship and help to countless numbers of people who have been privileged to glimpse Michael Ramsey's radiant spirituality which is never artificial, pompous or intense.

There was no incongruity in Michael Ramsey's being concurrently Canon of Durham Cathedral and Professor of Theology. For him there is no dichotomy between prayer and study. In his own student days at Cambridge he had been influenced deeply by his eminent teacher, Edwyn Hoskyns, a great New Testament scholar. In one of his Cambridge sermons Hoskyns had asked the students: 'Can we rescue a word, and discover a universe? Can we study a language, and awake to the truth? Can we bury ourselves in a lexicon and arise in the presence of God?' Michael Ramsey has always done just that. That is why, for him, to study the Bible is to discover a 'sparkling well of truth'.

Canon Ramsey was still only forty-six when he returned to Cambridge in 1950, this time as

Regius Professor of Divinity. In 1951 the University of Durham honoured him with an honorary DD, the first of some thirty universities to do likewise. Students flocked to his lectures and in Cambridge, as everywhere else, he was at his very best meeting large or small groups of students and answering their questions on a wide variety of topics. Those who were privileged to be his students in Lincoln, Durham and Cambridge had in Michael Ramsey a teacher who exemplified the patristic understanding of a theologian as 'one whose prayer is true'. Hardly had he established himself in the Regius Chair when the call came to be Bishop of Durham. So back to this most loved place he went in 1952.

In August 1952 Michael Ramsey rode his well-loved and ancient bicycle for the last time. This was not the only change in his metamorphosis from Regius Professor to Bishop. Bishop Ramsey has never been a man to wear his heart on his sleeve, but at the time it must have been a considerable sacrifice to give up the foremost academic post in the theological world. That the life of a bishop or a priest is essentially a life of personal sacrifice is a conviction that shines through many of Michael Ramsey's episcopal charges to his clergy in the dioceses of Durham, York and Canterbury, and in his books, especially *The Christian Priest Today*.

Bishop Michael Ramsey was in the line of the great scholar-bishops of Durham. His outspokenness was an advantage in the North, where he had great scope to demonstrate that theology and spirituality cannot be divorced either from each other or from their social context. He loved Durham and the diocese took him to its heart. As he went round the parishes, he was listened to by the industrialist and the miner as he had been by the scholar and the student. Years afterwards, when he had become Archbishop of Canterbury, the local newspaper was delighted to display a photograph of a barrel of beer being rolled into the Old Palace to entertain a coachload of miners who had come all the way from Sunderland to greet their old friend.

As a diocesan bishop Michael Ramsey showed exceptional powers of leadership and after four short years at Bishop Auckland he became Archbishop of York. And how greatly he loved the Minster! From a child he was intensely interested in church architecture and brass-rubbing, and all his life he has lived in the shadow of wonderful buildings – King's College Chapel, Ely Cathedral, the massive stones of Liverpool's new cathedral, the Boston 'Stump', Durham Cathedral, York Minster, Canterbury Cathedral. All of them have played their part in ordering and nourishing his own spiritual life, with its dual priorities of daily eucharistic worship and the daily recitation of Morning and Evening Prayer. Besides his height and dignified bearing and the dignity of his office, what made his presence in the long processions, great services and huge congregations so significant was his own sense of the numinous which communicated itself to others. The importance of liturgical worship in the life of an Anglican priest was one of his greatest emphases in his addresses to his clergy. In his old age and in the quiet seclusion of a small flat he prepares to say Evensong with his wife and any visitors as carefully and devoutly as if he were preparing for a service of several thousand people in a great cathedral, for he is just as surely 'entering into the courts of the Lord'. It is in liturgical prayer and worship that he fulfils pre-eminently the ancient precept of an Eastern monk: 'Put thy mind into thy heart and stand in the presence of God all the day long.' The rhythm of the Liturgy is supported by a disciplined pattern of contemplative and intercessory prayer.

In 1961, after only five years as Archbishop of York, Michael Ramsey became the hundredth Archbishop of Canterbury and the Primate of All England. He was to take a leading part in the theological conflicts of the next decade of which the 'Honest to God' debate was only a part. By his books and by his utterances he not only identified and clarified the major issues but gave outstanding theological leadership and pastoral guidance to clergy and laity alike. In his position as first of the lords spiritual he was brought into frequent contact with royalty, with the peers of the realm, with Ministers of State and with persons of position and influence in all walks of life. He had always maintained his interest in, and grasp of, world affairs since his youthful participation in politics and debating societies. In the many speeches and pronouncements he was called upon to make it was evident that his was a spirituality formed of prophetic vision, fearless courage and moral responsibility.

Throughout his primacy he worked tirelessly to

bring about closer relations between the Anglican Church, the Church of Rome, the Orthodox Churches and the Churches of the Reformation. For him the quest for unity could not be pursued in isolation from the quest for truth and holiness. He was an indefatigable traveller who did his best to visit, as the father of a worldwide family of churches, every part of the Anglican Communion, some parts of it many times. Whether at home or abroad, whether among the churches of the Anglican Communion or in debate and fellowship with other Christian churches, Michael Ramsey's whole life and worship has been built on the theological perception and spiritual experience of the Church as an integral part of the Gospel, a body 'whose maker and builder is God'.

In a broadcast address from Jarrow to commemorate the thirteen-hundredth anniversary of the birth of the Venerable Bede, Bishop Michael recalled how, throughout his life, Bede 'prayed, and he prayed and he prayed; and he read, and he read and he read; and he wrote, and he wrote and he wrote'. In describing the contribution of Bede to English Christianity Michael Ramsey might have been giving us a self-portrait. In all his manifold activity he never forgot, and never allowed those committed to his charge to forget, the goal of our earthly existence. In 1970 he reminded a student audience in Cambridge, and reminds all who read this book, that the goal of our earthly pilgrimage is no less than the quest of heaven and that the road to it is the road of selfless love:

'Do not be afraid of looking towards heaven,

for heaven is the meaning of our existence as created in God's likeness for fellowship with him. And the quest of heaven is very far from being a pious escapism, inasmuch as the essence of heaven is selfless love, the same love which drives you to go without your dinner to help a family which has no food at all.'*

In his increasingly less active retirement Bishop Michael continues to show us that Christian spirituality is wholeness, as well as holiness, of life; and it is this unity of prayer, thought and life as the bedrock of his spiritual wisdom that this book seeks to demonstrate.

LORNA KENDALL
Canterbury
Kent

Freedom, Faith and the Future (SPCK 1970).

The Christian hope

The first hope of every Christian is the hope of heaven: the first, the nearest, the most relevant of his hopes. Does that surprise you?

Is heaven a possibility too far away for immediate thought? No . . . man exists in order to have the most intimate relation with God that is possible; a relationship of fellowship and indeed friendship mingled with awe and dependence.

To give glory to God, in the biblical phrase, is to enjoy that fellowship, to come to reflect God's own character of outgoing love and humbly to have God and not one's self as the centre. There lies man's true status, true freedom and true destiny.

Do not be afraid of looking towards heaven, for heaven is the meaning of our existence as created in God's likeness for fellowship with him.

And the quest of heaven is very far from being a pious escapism, inasmuch as the essence of heaven is selfless love, the same love which drives you to go without your dinner to help a family which has no food at all.

The glory of God and the Christian faith

The glory of God illuminates every part of the structure of the Christian faith:

God
The glory of God has been disclosed in his created works. To glorify God is both to rejoice in his works, and to own their absolute dependence upon the Creator.

Incarnation
It was in humiliation that the glory was revealed on earth. The mission of the Lord was at once the descent of one who trod the road of frustration, ignorance, pain and death, and the ascent of one who was realizing in humiliation a glory which had been his from all eternity.

Atonement
The glory shown forth on Calvary was a kingly power mightier than the human and cosmic evil which was ranged against it. The prince of this world was defeated and judged: the world was overcome.

Church
The glory which Christians are to grow into and to manifest by the practical response to the Christian life is a glory which is Christ's and which *is theirs* already.

The wisdom of God in creation

The wisdom of God is working through all created life, and far and wide is the sustainer and the inspirer of the thought and the endeavour of men.

The Church will therefore reverence every honest activity of the minds of men; it will perceive that therein the Spirit of God is moving, and it will tremble lest by denying this, in word or in action, it blaspheme the Spirit of God.

But wisdom cannot be thus learnt in all its fullness. The mind and the eye of man are distorted by sin and self-worship; and the wisdom which the Spirit of God unfolds throughout the world can lead to blindness and to deceit unless men face the fact of sin and the need for redemption.

The wisdom of God in the cross

The Church proclaims the wisdom of God, set forth in its very essence in the crucifixion of Jesus Christ, a wisdom learnt when men are brought to the crisis of repentance and to the resulting knowledge of self and of God.

The wisdom of the cross seems at first to deny the wisdom of the Spirit of God in the created world; it scandalizes men's sense of the good and the beautiful.

But the Christians, who have first faced the scandal, discover in the cross a key to the meaning of all creation. The cross unlocks its secrets and its sorrows, and interprets them in terms of the power of God.

The cross is the place where the theology of the Church has its meaning, where the unity of the Church is a deep and present reality, and where the Church is already showing the peace of God and the bread from heaven to the nations of mankind.

The wisdom of God in the Church

The wisdom uttered in the cross has created the Church and is expressed through the Church's whole life as the Body of Christ crucified and risen.

The Church's work in thinking and interpreting and teaching is inseparable from the Church's life in Christ. Its authority is Christ himself, known in the building-up of the one Body in truth and in love. Hence 'orthodoxy' means not only 'right opinion', but also 'right worship' or 'true glory', after the biblical meaning of the word *'doxa'*; for life and thought and worship are inseparable activities in the Body of Christ.

But as Jesus in the midst of his works of healing and feeding was moving towards death, so also is his Church. For the Church exists for something deeper than philanthropy and reform, namely to teach men to die to self and to trust in a resurrection to a new life which, because it spans both this world and another world, can never be wholly understood here, and must always puzzle the world's idealists. Hence, as the Body of Christ crucified and risen, the Church points men to a unity and a peace which men generally neither understand nor desire.

The Kingdom of God

Jesus sets forth the reign of God as the purpose of God being accomplished in the whole range of the life of man, bodily as well as spiritual.

As we see this total programme of the Kingdom of God we realize that in the mind of Jesus the bodily health of man, though so very important, is not an end in itself; it is but one part of the life of man which exists to do God's will and reflect his righteousness and his love.

Thus we find Jesus, as the story proceeds, more and more withdrawing from his work of healing, even though it is a work so utterly near to his heart, and concentrating upon the paramount theme of sin and the forgiveness of sin. And it is in the realm of sin and forgiveness and the establishment of righteousness that the central core of the reign of God is going to be established.

Again and again Jesus insists that all men must repent, all men must pray, 'forgive us our sins'; and forgiveness is among the great gifts which Jesus brings.

The Kingdom is in a wonderful way embodied in himself and in his own person. Where he is, there is God's reign; and being with him and accepting him is accepting God's reign.

God is Christlike

The importance of the confession 'Jesus is Lord' is not only that Jesus is divine but that God is Christlike. 'God is Christlike and in him is no unChristlikeness at all.'

The Christlikeness of God means that his passion and resurrection are the key to the very meaning of God's own deity. Is there within and beyond the universe any coherence or meaning or pattern or sovereignty? The New Testament doctrine is that in the death and resurrection of Jesus, in the fact of living through dying, of finding life through losing it, of the saving of self through the giving of self, there is this sovereignty. And to believe it with more than a bare intellectual consent is to believe it existentially, and to believe it existentially is to follow the way of finding life through losing it.

Every coming of the power of God into the world happens through pain and cost, and every growth in our own holiness and Christlikeness happens also through pain and cost. The grace of God can turn the pain and cost to wonderful account, and we pray that the evil one may not use them for his evil ends.

Jesus, God and man

When God became incarnate as man his meaning-fulness as God came into its own. The self-giving, the becoming-man, the suffering love were not additions to the divine experience or mere incidents in the divine history. In becoming man, God revealed the meaning of what it is to be God. The glory is seen in the becoming-man because it is a glory 'beyond' and eternal.

So, too, in Jesus the human race finds its own true meaning. Men rejected Jesus because they preferred the glory of man to the glory of God, as St John draws out in his Gospel.

Man's true glory is the reflection in him of the divine glory, the self-giving love seen in Jesus.

Thus it is in Jesus that we see man becoming his true self, in that giving away of self which happens when man is possessed by God. The meaning of what it is to be man appears when man is the place where deity fulfils himself, and the glory of the one is the glory of the other. The phrase 'the Man for others' is an illuminating one, but it is not the whole story, for God created man not only for others but for God.

Jesus, the living Lord

Jesus, the living Lord. What does it all mean for humanity down the ages?

'The Word became flesh and dwelt among us and we beheld – we saw – his glory.' Now that is terribly familiar – the Gospel every Christmas Day. But step back and look what an astonishing statement it is.

'Word', 'flesh', both are biblical terms with a very distinct meaning.
'Word': that denotes One who is living, active, Creator divine.
'Flesh': that, as a biblical term, denotes the opposite. Flesh means that which is mortal, frail, perishing, destined to die. Now the contrast is between one who is divine, sharing the divine life of the Creator himself – the Living One – and human life viewed in all its creatureliness and frailty and mortality.

The total meaning is that in this happening the Word became flesh; one who is divine took upon himself genuinely our frail, creaturely human existence.

Jesus is Lord:
We believe in the historic life of a person 2000 years ago.
We confess his deity as the early believers confessed his deity.
Jesus is of the present as well as the past: he is; he still is.

The sparkling well of truth

We hold together Jesus portrayed in the Gospels and Jesus as the living Lord in the midst of his people today: Jesus in the Bible, Jesus in the Blessed Sacrament.

But the doctrine of Christ means far more than the historic Jesus.

We have given to us the pattern of belief set out in the Creed, from 'God the Father Almighty' right through to 'the resurrection of the body and the life of the world to come'. Do not treat the doctrines of the Creed as a string of impersonal items, like a row of bricks picked out of a box. Treat them as doctrines of Christ, as so many aspects of the mystery of which he is the centre.

Thus the Father Almighty declares his almighty power most chiefly in showing mercy and pity – in the mercy and pity of Christ's incarnation. Again, the Holy Catholic Church is Christ's family, Christ's household. The Communion of Saints is the company of those who reflect Christ's glory, and heaven is the enjoyment of Christ's radiance. See Christian doctrine in this way, and it will make all the difference to your study of it.

Think of study rather as being refreshed from the deep, sparkling well of truth which is Christ himself.

The transfiguration of Christ

The transfiguration of Christ stands as a gateway to the saving events of the Gospel, and is as a mirror in which the Christian mystery is seen in its unity.

But the transfiguration meant the taking of the whole conflict of the Lord's mission, just as it was, into the glory which gave meaning to it all.

Confronted as he is with a universe more than ever terrible in the blindness of its processes and the destructiveness of its potentialities mankind must be led to the Christian faith not as a panacea of progress nor as an other-worldly solution unrelated to history, but as a gospel of transfiguration. Such a gospel both transcends the world and speaks to the immediate here-and-now. He who is transfigured is the Son of Man; and, as he discloses on Mount Hermon another world, he reveals that no part of created things and no moment of created time lies outside the power of the Spirit, who is Lord, to change from glory into glory.

The riches of Christ

'Being rich he became poor, that you through his poverty might be rich' (2 Corinthians 8:9).

The riches which Christ would share with us are his glory, his power and his joy.

Christ's glory is the self-giving love seen in his life and death. He would share that with us, and he indeed shares it with us in the Blessed Sacrament today. Christ's power was the kind of power men found it hard to understand: not the power of privilege and lording it over people, but the more subtle power of loving influence, of the winning of minds and consciences to the truth.

We who are Christians are called to make Christ's glory our own and Christ's power our own. And with these gifts there comes his joy.

Come to Bethlehem once again. See the stable, see the child. And knowing that he is God made Man, knowing that he who is rich has become poor for us, we can kneel in the darkness and the cold which is the symbol of our cold and chilly human race and say, with a grasp we may never have had before, the doxology at the end of the Lord's Prayer: 'Yours is the kingdom, and the power and the glory for ever.'

The tears of Jesus unite our world

Again and again I find the apostles in the New Testament writings bidding the Christians of their time to think of the greater conflicts, the greater hardships of their brethren in other lands. We are, we really are, members of one another.

Am I ready for a simpler way of life? Do I myself care enough to be doing all I can in the service of the hungry? Do I care in a way that really costs me?

We may picture Jesus today weeping over many cities, towns, villages and countries: some with their poverty and hunger, some with their wealth, their power and their complacency.

The tears of Jesus unite our world and show us how bound in a bundle we are. Jesus would have us share in his grief, and if we are his followers we shall not wish it otherwise. But those who share in the grief of Jesus are admitted to a share in his joy: his joy over one sinner who mends his ways, his joy over every cup of cold water given to a child who is in need, his joy over every act of true service to his heavenly Father and to mankind.

We shall not ask, 'Who is my neighbour?' My neighbour is Christ and Christ is everywhere.

Reading St John

How shall we set about our reading? St John's Gospel gives us a picture of the life and teaching of Jesus by a disciple who had pondered its meaning and who came to understand its message for the human race. This book shows us Jesus as he was experienced, known and loved centuries ago. But in our reading we shall not only be looking back. We shall be thinking again and again how this same Jesus is alive today and speaking to us now as he spoke to Nathaniel and Nicodemus and the woman of Samaria. We read of Jesus as they saw him and heard him centuries ago. We know that this same Jesus is present with us and speaking directly to us through the deeds and words of which we read.

We shall be praying: 'Lord Jesus, as I read the Gospel of your disciple, show me what I shall hear and receive and do. Make this Gospel a living word to me.'

The feet-washing

John 13:1–16

Notice the words with which the evangelist introduces the feet-washing scene. 'Jesus, knowing that the Father had given all things into his hands, and that he had come from God and was going to God . . .' He washed their feet as one to whom divine authority completely belonged. He is showing to the disciples and to us what the divine glory is really like.

What is the glory of God really like? The glory of the infinite and eternal God who rules and sustains the universe? Men had longed to know. Now the veil is drawn aside: the glory of God is like Jesus washing the feet of the disciples. It is the glory of a God who humbles himself. Think how God humbles himself in his relations to the world, in the humble birth in the manger at Bethlehem, in Calvary, in all his gentle and patient dealings with ourselves. In that humility of God we see what the glory of God is like.

Our worship means humbling ourselves before the God who is himself humble.

The things to come

John 14:12–20

The departure of Jesus to death will enable the coming of a new relationship between Jesus and the disciples.

Prayer in the name of Jesus is sure to be answered, and to pray in the name of Jesus is to pray as people who are possessed by him. The Holy Spirit, coming to be their Advocate and their Comforter, will enable these things to happen. Jesus will not show himself to all the world, but those who love him and keep his words will have Jesus and the Father coming and making their dwelling within them.

All this will be made possible because Jesus is going to his death. The disciples will lose the present relation to Jesus of sight and touch in order to enter upon the unseen relation to him in the future. Let them be glad in what is happening. Meanwhile the conflict is imminent, the prince of evil is approaching. It is time to go, and Jesus says, 'Let us go on.'

The prayer for glory

John 17:1–5

Jesus prays that on the coming day which is Good Friday, the Father will give glory to him and he will give glory to the Father. The glory is the splendour of self-giving love, and this glory is God's in all eternity in the self-giving love of Father and Son in the power of the Spirit.

Now it is going to be revealed in the midst of suffering and death, a suffering and death so real that Jesus has shrunk from it and will shrink from it again; but the Father's will and glory are paramount and in that will and glory he shares.

It has been the work of Jesus in his mission to give the life eternal to those who believe and this life eternal is the life lived here and now in the knowledge of God and of Jesus. In this way the disciples of Jesus are having a glimpse of the things which are eternal, and when Jesus passes on to suffering and death he has eternity in his heart.

The prayer for unity

John 17:16–19

Jesus now prays for his immediate disciples. It is
for them to show his love and truth to the world,
and he prays that they may be kept in the truth
he has revealed and in the holiness in which he
has consecrated himself on their own behalf. The
prayer for their unity is linked with the prayer
for their faithfulness to the truth and for their
consecration in holiness.

The prayer has often been called the prayer of
Jesus for unity. It is no less the prayer for truth
and for holiness. Indeed, it is being increasingly
realized that the recovery of true unity among
Christians cannot be separated from their deeper
realization of the truth and from their growth in
a deeper holiness. Pope John's vision of the
renewal of Christians as the key to the unity of
Christians means that Christians, by being drawn
far closer to Christ in the way of holiness, become
more effectively close to one another.

We pray: 'Eternal and merciful God, have mercy
upon thy Church and grant that we seeking unity
in Christ and in the truth of the holy word may,
with one mind and one mouth, glorify thee, the
Father of Jesus Christ our Lord.'

The prayer for disciples to come

John 17:20–25

Jesus goes on to pray for those who will in future
become disciples. It is a prayer which includes
ourselves. He prays that we may be one with one
another by sharing in the oneness of the Father
and the Son. He prays that we may share now in
the glory of the passion and so come to share in
the glory of Jesus in heaven and see it with our
eyes.

Jesus is on his way imminently to Gethsemane and
Calvary, and yet heaven is near. Indeed, the deeper
he plunges into the world's darkness the nearer
he is to heaven. This is because love is one and
indivisible, and the love which will suffer and die
on earth is the same love which reigns eternally.
The prayer of Jesus has been reflected in saintly
men and women through the centuries who have
suffered greatly and yet have found their suffering
already transfigured by heavenly light.

We pray: 'O God, whose beloved Son went not
up to joy but first he suffered pain, nor to his
glory before embracing the cross: plant his cross
in our hearts, that in its power and love we may
come to the end of our faith and a heavenly crown,
through the same Jesus Christ our Lord.'

To Calvary

John 19:17–23

As in the Garden, soon on Calvary, while St Mark shows the darkness and the loneliness, St John shows the glory. There is no inconsistency. It is in the utter self-giving of Jesus to loneliness and death that the glory shines.

Majestically, Jesus carries his own cross, and he walks as one who has power to lay down his life, and power to take it again. Pilate, in a final bout of obstinacy, insists upon the title on the cross being 'the King of the Jews', and the writing of this in Hebrew and Latin and Greek is a symbol of the proclamation of the kingship of Jesus to all nations. 'Tell it out among the heathen that the Lord is King.' We remember the Greeks who came on Palm Sunday and said, 'Sir, we would see Jesus', and Jesus had spoken of the lifting-up drawing all men to himself. Many Greeks and people of every race will be drawing near to Calvary in the coming centuries.

The victory

John 19:28–30

'It is finished.'

Here is not a defeat which needs the resurrection to reverse it. Rather is it a victory so signal that Easter comes quickly to seal it. The victory concerns both sin and suffering.

Sin has done its worst, but here is righteousness undefeated. Suffering has done its worst, but Jesus has so used it as to transfigure it.

The glory is here, and for all time sinners and sufferers may in faith draw upon the victory of Jesus: sin conquered, suffering transfigured. In the Epistle of John we read, 'This is the victory that overcomes the world, our faith' (1 John 5:4).

'We pray for faith in Christ's victory. Pray that sufferers known to you may have its comfort.'

Easter

John 20:1–10

Jesus has been raised, and raised to a new and glorious mode of being. But just as the incarnation and the whole mission of Jesus is not spiritual only, so the resurrection is not spiritual only. It is the beginning of God's re-creation of the world that he has made. That was the faith of the apostolic church.

But there could be no lingering at the tomb. The resurrection brings a new order. Mary Magdalene must not cling, she must go and tell the disciples that Jesus is on his way to ascend to heaven.

The disciples, rejoicing in the presence of Jesus on Easter evening, are sent on their mission to the world as Jesus himself had been sent by the Father.

So all are to look forward.

The Holy Spirit

The Spirit, poured out on the day of Pentecost, is the gift of the crucified and exalted Jesus. The Spirit is the Spirit of Jesus. That is the revolution in the concept of Spirit which appears in the early Church.

That St Luke in Acts sees the rise of Christianity as a drama of the Holy Spirit is clear.

The Church exists by the power of the Holy Spirit. Whether as fellowship, or body, or temple, or people of God, it has no existence apart from the impact of the Holy Spirit upon human lives.

The Spirit's renewal of the Church is linked with the Spirit's witness to the life, death and resurrection of Jesus. The way of truth along which the Paraclete leads is always the way that is Christ himself, as he takes the things of Christ and declares them to the disciples.

But it is a costly thing to invoke the Spirit, for the glory of Calvary was the cost of the Spirit's mission and is the cost of the Spirit's renewal. It is in the shadow of the cross that in any age of history Christians pray: 'Come, thou holy Paraclete.'

The Holy Spirit and the world

Spirit is not a thing-in-itself, or a person-in-himself, or a philosophical entity in itself; it means that God himself is active in the world.

As the action of Christ in the Church includes the Spirit's kindling of the believers' responses, so the action of the Word in the world will include the Spirit's kindling of human responses.

For the world's salvation it is the work of the Holy Spirit not only to produce goodness in human lives but to lead human lives to acknowledge God as the author of goodness and to glorify Christ.

Three issues are raised by the relation of the Spirit in the *ecclesia* and the Spirit in the world: the sciences, the world religions, the diffused goodness in the world.

Each of these three issues calls for the uninhibited recognition of the divine Word, and therefore Spirit, in the world, and also for the acknowledgement of a divine Saviour without whom neither science, nor religion, nor goodness, can climb to heaven — for heaven is the perfect sharing in the glory of God through the Spirit.

The Church and the glory of Christ

'And the glory which thou hast given me, I have given unto them; that they may be one, even as we are one' (John 18:22).

Herein lies the meaning of the Church. It is the mystery of the participation of men and women in the glory which is Christ's. Baptized into his death and made sharers in his resurrection they are members of the Body which is Christ's, branches of the vine who is Christ.

Inasmuch as the glory dwells in it, the Church is the temple of God. But the glory in the Church is an invisible glory. Though the Church is visible, the glory is not to be confused with earthly majesty and splendour, for it is a glory discernible without and realized within – only through faith.

Only at the parousia will the glory become visible. The glory in the Church is but a foretaste of the glory that is to come. *Here* the powers of the age to come are at work within the Church's humiliation: *there* the open vision of a glory awaits the Church in the day when judgement will begin at the house of God. Torn from this eschatological context the doctrine of the Church becomes the doctrine of an institution among other institutions upon the plane of history.

The holy tradition and the Bible

Tradition does not mean that the Church has teachings which supplement those of the Bible or constitute an additional corpus of revelation. It means rather that it is within the common life, the worship and the general mind of the Christian community that the Christian is attuned to the understanding of the biblical message.

Tradition will be our guide to the interpretation of the Bible through the appeal to the total life and experience of the Church from the ancient Fathers onwards.

Tradition will be recovered not as a petrified catena of doctrinal norms, but as the lively activity of the Christian community, its members serving one another and serving the world and so being the corporate scene in which the message of the Bible is dynamically felt and understood. The common life of the Church will interpret the Bible not as the protector of its contents so much as the divine–human encounter in which the Word of God is heard.

It is through this work of interpretation that the Bible's own history and categories become not less but more authoritative as declaring the meaning of God and the meaning of man.

The holy tradition: why do we look to the age of the Fathers?

Amidst totally different cultural scenes, calling as they do for new understandings, why do we look back to the age of the Fathers? We learn what we can from any and every Christian century, but we look back to the time of the Fathers because it tells us of the historical givenness of our faith and because of the continuing identity of the Holy Catholic Church.

It matters greatly that the Fathers took seriously issues about truth which are still with us. It matters that the God who is the world's Saviour is also the world's Creator, and it matters that this God does not send a sort of intermediary to bring salvation to the world but gives his own very self to unite humanity to himself.

But the appeal of Christians to history is not a mere journey into the past, for the past is living and its saints are near and with us in the family which unites earth to heaven and heaven to earth.

Athanasius and Basil and Chrysostom, together with Ambrose and Augustine and Leo, are with us in this family. We share with them and with the Mother of our Lord and God in heaven's own worship, and they are with us as we witness to our Saviour in a dark and stormy world.

The holy tradition: the way of the mystics

Mysticism in the proper sense is an intense realization of God within the self and the self embraced within God in vivid nearness.

It is a phenomenon known in a number of religions, and in those religions very similar language is used in describing the experience. There is deep darkness, the darkness of not knowing; and there is light with flashes in which the self knows the unknowable terribly near and knows itself as never before.

Now through the centuries Christian teaching has emphasized that the significant thing is not just the mystic experience in itself but its place and its context within the whole life of a Christian. The experience is given by God sometimes to one who seeks God in a life of humility and charity, turned towards the righteousness as well as the beauty of God. And the effect of the experience of mystic union, sometimes described as 'passive contemplation', is not to cause the person to long to have the experience again but to long to serve God and to do his will.

Those who have had mystic experience will not want to tell everyone about it: they will have a longing to serve God in daily life, for in his *will* is our peace.

Mystic experience is given to some. But contemplation is for all Christians.

The holy tradition in the Anglican Church

I believe that the holy tradition is living in our Church: for what is holy tradition but the continuous stream of divine life, which is the very life of God Incarnate and of the Holy Spirit within the Church?

This divine life is in the Scriptures, the preaching of the Gospel, the Sacraments, the lives of Christians, the fellowship of the Saints. Such is the holy tradition.

In our Anglican theology we do not speak of it precisely as the Orthodox do. But it is there, with us and in us. We ascribe to Holy Scripture a supreme right to check and test what properly belongs to holy tradition and what does not.

We need to give thought to the relation between the Church as eternal and the Church as embodied in the movement of history, and also to the relation between divine truth and the words in which divine truth is embodied.

Theological work, prayer, liturgy, friendship and action together to meet the world's distresses, all these are part of the way to unity.

The holy tradition is God Incarnate living and moving in the whole life of Christians.

The historic Church and the Church of the future

The language of structure is but one among the metaphors for the Church, and all the metaphors need to be seen together: building, body, vine, *ecclesia*.

Each of the metaphors speaks of the once-for-all givenness of the Church and each of them speaks also of the growth of the Church in its way to becoming perfectly what it is. Into the metaphor of the temple, for instance, there bursts another metaphor, for the stones of the temple are *living* stones.

We cherish the gift of historic faith and order not as the walls of an enclosed fortress but as gifts of God which both witness to the past and serve the building of a future as yet unrealized. By thus combining the historical and the futuristic notes in our understanding of the Church we may be helped in our efforts to combine a loyalty to tradition with a sensitivity to contemporary movements.

If this is a difficult adventure it is not one which need endanger our souls. Rather might our souls be endangered if we were content either to rest in past tradition undisturbed or to share in contemporary enthusiasms without relation to the stream of Christian witness through the ages.

The Church and the world

The Church will follow Christ in the outgoing service of human needs, the poor, the hungry, the sick, the disinherited, with no motive but the compassion drawn from Christ himself and with the humility which banishes patronage or possessiveness.

The Church needs to be challenging the world's assumptions and showing that the world's greatest need is to be brought in humility and repentance into the love and obedience of God.

Amidst its deep involvement in the service of the community the Church will keep alive for its own members, and strive to keep alive for others, three unchanging evangelical themes:

The first is the priority of *divine forgiveness* as providing the keynote of Christian ethics. The Christian community is the forgiven community; that is the ground of its relation to God and of the humility of its service of man.

The second theme is *heaven*. Heaven gives meaning to our existence now; defines the infinite worth of every man, woman and child; and provides the perspective in which life's problems are seen.

The third theme is *worship*. It will be a worship that is not apart from the life of the world but set right in the heart of that life, a practice of adoration and contemplation in the midst of the world's busyness.

The Christian priest today

Slaves of Christ and servants of men. Can we recapture the truth and wonder of this vocation?

First, the priest is one who learns theology and teaches it. His study is deep and constant, not that he may be erudite but that he may be simple.

While he teaches the laity what they do not know without his help, he must all the while be learning from them about the questions to which theology is applied.

Next, the priest represents in the life of the Church the dimension of a Divine Reconciliation. He will find himself but one of many agencies who help distressed souls with various skills and techniques. But amidst them all it will be for him to represent the often-forgotten dimension of God's forgiveness of the contrite.

So, too, the priest will be in a special way the Man of Prayer.

The work of a pastor is a work of prayer with its own intensity of sorrow and joy.

Lastly, and in a way which sums up all, the priest is the Man of the Eucharist.

His office represents that dimension of the more than local, the more than contemporary, which is the true context of the rite in the Gospel and in the Church Catholic.

The Communion of Saints

Our deeper realization of the Communion of
Saints turns not only upon our understanding of
the saints but upon our understanding of the
nature of prayer.

If our prayer is shaped by our own needs and
requests then we may slip into thinking of the
saints as those who answer our prayers by dispen-
sing favours to us. If, however, our prayer is
shaped by the giving of glory to God in the quest
of his will and his Kingdom, then we may be lifted
out of ourselves in the company of those who in
paradise and heaven seek that glory and reflect it.

Within the family of the saints we may ask the
prayers of those who are near to the vision of
God, and we may pray for all in earth or paradise
or heaven. But we do not forget that the family
includes those who are weak and struggling like
ourselves, and those whose saintliness is very faint
because the world has been reclaiming them. Our
prayer looks towards the weak as well as towards
the strong, and if we are faithful it will reach both
ways since the glory of Christ is always one with
the agony of his compassion. Such is the meaning
of 'I believe in the Communion of Saints'.

What are we here for?

Is there in our divided and frustrated world anywhere a clue, a meaning, a pattern, a sovereignty, a way? And Christianity answers: Yes, there is a clue, a meaning, a pattern, a sovereignty, a way; and this is depicted in the parable of Jesus about the corn of wheat which dies in order to be fruitful. It is thus that God conquers evil. And wherever in the world there are lives which so live, there a light is shining reflecting Christ's own light, and there a trail is blazed.

So we salute the saints.

It is not *doing good* in the world that makes a saint; he does often do good, but so do many people whom we would never call saints. No, the saint is one who has a strange nearness to God and makes God real and near to other people. He embodies the parable of the corn of wheat that falls into the earth and dies.

The saints reflect Jesus in the world. They answer the question-mark of the bewildered who ask, Where is the clue? What is the goal? What is the world for? They show us what *we* are here for — 'unless a grain of wheat falls to the earth and dies . . .'

Why was the world created? All Saints' Day gives the answer.

Sin and forgiveness

Amidst all the various activities for the putting right of human ills there is so often a whole dimension missing, the dimension of sin and forgiveness.

It is this dimension of sin and forgiveness which the priest keeps alive by an office which represents the forgiving Church and the forgiving Lord Jesus. He will do this by his ministry in Confession and Absolution and by his preaching of the gospel of God's reconciliation.

The faith of the disciples did in the event fail and it was restored in a new depth. It may therefore be that the Father's response to the request of Jesus was to allow the loyalty of disciples to fail in the certainty that through their failure they will be freed from self-reliance and brought to a faith that is a true death to self.

If theology would avoid the dangers of a false secularization the sure safeguard is to keep at its heart the essential Christian attitudes of creature to Creator, of sinner to Saviour. It is when we have lost the attitude of the worshipper, of awe and reverence in the presence of the Other, and when we have ceased to ask forgiveness for our sins, that the line has been crossed. It is on this line that the crisis for secular Christianity is located.

Sacramental confession

As absolver the priest shares, on the one hand, in the broken heart of sin and penitence and, on the other hand, in the sorrow and joy of Christ who bears our sins and pardons them.

Every priest should know enough of psychology to realize how little he knows, and to recognize those instances where he should advise recourse to a psychiatrist. But there are the many occasions where the priest can help the penitent by his knowledge of spirituality together with practical wisdom and sympathy.

Many find that the significance of sacramental confession for them may change through the passing of time. A first confession may be an occasion of vivid realization of the cross and a decisive turning-point in spiritual depth. Subsequent confessions in the early years can have a like vividness.

Then a time may come when the vividness fades and confession seems to have the staleness of a humdrum discipline. It is when going to confession requires a sheer discipline of the will that you may find in new ways how the loving kindness of God can hide, as it were, beneath the recesses of your failure, and you are humbled by discovering how God can use you in spite of yourself. Your humility and your grateful trust in him are renewed.

How may we think of heaven?

How may we think of heaven?

In his work *The City of God* St Augustine told of heaven thus: 'We shall rest and we shall see, we shall see and we shall love, we shall love and we shall praise, in the end which is no end.'

Rest: we shall be freed from the busy and fussy activity in which we get in our own light and expose ourselves to our self-centredness.

Resting, we shall find that we see in a new way, without the old hindrances. We shall see our neighbours as what they really are, creatures and children of God in whom is the divine image, and that image will become newly visible to us. We shall see ourselves too as God's infinitesimally small creatures: and we shall begin to see God himself in his beauty.

Seeing, we shall love, for how shall we not love God in his beauty and how shall we not love all our neighbours in whom the image of God is now visible to us?

Praise will be the last word, for all is of God and none is of our own achievement, and we shall know the depth of gratitude and adoration.

Such is the heaven for which we were created.

The true life of man on earth

Resting, seeing, loving and praising: these words describe not only the goal of heaven but the message of Christianity in the world.

The world has lost the way of resting, seeing, loving, praising. Swept along in ceaseless activity the world does not pause to consider. With no resting and no considering the power to see is lost: to see where we are going, to see the larger perspectives, to see beyond the group or the nation or the race, to see human beings as they really are with the image of God in them. Where seeing is dim, love becomes faint; and praise is lost for we praise only when first we have seen and loved. Man loses the praise of his Creator which is the end of his existence and the source of his resting, seeing and loving.

If the words 'rest, see, love, praise' tell both of heaven and of the true life of man on earth, they tell no less of the Church's renewal.

The renewal of the Church will mean a rest which is exposed to the darkness and light of contemplation, a seeing of both the heavenly perspective and the distresses of the world, a loving which passes into costly service, and a praising which is from the depth of the soul.

The praise of God's glory

God has declared his glory to the end that all creation may give glory to him.

When men glorify God they do not add to his glory, they acknowledge it.

The perfect act of worship is seen only in the Son of Man. By him alone there is made the perfect acknowledgement upon earth of the glory of God and the perfect response to it.

At the heart of the Church's glorifying of God there is the new rite of the Eucharist. Here the Church is united to the glory of Christ on Calvary and in heaven, and finds the focus of the glorifying of God by all created things.

It is not to be thought that the Gospel will be made simple to the worldly and impenitent, and the attempt to make it simple to them may corrupt or distort it. The Gospel of the glory of God is always very near to mankind, and yet always very far from them: near, because the divine image is in mankind and the Gospel is the true meaning of man; far, because it is heard only by a faith and a repentance which overthrow all man's glorying in himself and his works.

The prayer of Jesus

It seems right to infer that the prayer of Jesus, a great while before day, was an intimate part of the work of that day.

For Jesus as for the disciples prayer is of the essence of the work of God.

On Calvary Mark and Matthew tell only of the prayer of desolation. Luke, whose account lessens the sense of loneliness by telling of the compassion of Jesus reaching out to those around him, records other prayers of Jesus on Calvary. Jesus prays for the soldiers who crucify him, commending them to the Father's compassion: 'Father, forgive them; for they know not what they do' (Luke 23:34).

Finally, omitting the cry of desolation, Luke tells of Jesus committing himself to the Father in death: 'Father, into thy hands I commend my spirit.' Obedience to the Father, thanksgiving to the Father, intimacy with the Father have marked the mission of Jesus from first to last.

Such is the prayer of Jesus in his life on earth as the traditions in the first three Gospels describe it. His prayer is the prayer of one who is deeply one with the Father while he shares in the frustrations of humanity.

The Lord's Prayer

In the Lord's Prayer the whole meaning of prayer is summed up.

But the Lord's Prayer cannot be understood apart from the whole ministry and teaching of Jesus. Its significance is unfolded as Jesus moves forward in his work for men; for in this work, and above all in his death and resurrection, there is revealed the meaning of the words around which the Lord's Prayer centres — the Father, the name, the Kingdom, the will.

The key-words of the Lord's Prayer set before us a picture of the whole work of Jesus Christ, and to pray the Lord's Prayer in his name we must leave Galilee and go up to Jerusalem, where we see the Father's name and Kingdom and will expressed in the passion.

In short the basis of Christian prayer is not the Lord's Prayer alone, but the Lord's Prayer and the Lord. Prayer in his name means prayer through all that he is and all that he has done.

Hence, if we would pray the Lord's Prayer aright, we must use it in the light of its interpretation in the whole of the New Testament.

Jesus: the ladder of Christian prayer

Christian prayer means not only the Lord's Prayer but the Lord's Prayer and the Lord.

The praying Christian is one whose prayer is uniquely his own, a divine and human movement within his own soul and nowhere else; and as no two people are the same, so the prayer of no two people is the same. But solitary as prayer may be, it is always interwoven with the prayer of Jesus, the prayer of the Holy Spirit within, and the praying family of the Church in every place.

Christian prayer is indeed a ladder, and the top of it reaches to heaven.

But the ladder of Christian prayer not only reaches to heaven and rests most firmly on earth. More than that, it unites heaven and earth very closely, because the ladder is Jesus, the Incarnate Lord.

In him, through him, we share today in the prayers and praises of the blessed saints in heaven. In him, through him, we touch with our prayers the sins and sorrows of mankind. And in him, through him, our prayers shall be made one in him, as he is in the Father in the bond of the Holy Ghost.

Liturgical worship

If the Lord's Prayer and the phrase 'through Jesus Christ' be interpreted in the whole light of the New Testament, then clearly Christian prayer is primarily neither mystical nor prophetic in its essence, but *liturgical*. It is the sharing by men in the one action of Christ, through their dying to their own egotisms as they are joined in one Body with his death and resurrection.

The regular and ordered movement of Liturgy is not a cumbrous addition to Christian prayer; rather does it express the New Testament fact of worship as the divine action into which all spontaneous and congregational prayer is ever merged.

Furthermore, the fellowship which we are building up in our parishes is a fellowship between us who live on earth and the Church in paradise and in heaven. This dimension of fellowship needs constant emphasis, and a fuller liturgical expression such as it had in the First Prayer Book of King Edward VI. Happy are those whose churches are full of reminders that the Church on earth is a colony of heaven, and that those who are called to be saints have fellowship with the glorious saints already.

The Liturgy of the Word

In spite of the utter newness of the access to the Father through Jesus in one Spirit which the new covenant has brought, the worship of the new *ecclesia* has a real continuity with the worship of the old. It is the same God of glory who is worshipped.

Within the new *ecclesia* the Scriptures of the old *ecclesia* are retained as Holy Scriptures, for they are now seen to speak of Christ and his glory. Among these Scriptures the Psalter has its special place.

The Psalter is used in the Church with a twofold rationale:

1   It is the voice of the Israel of God, worshipping now as of old the Creator, King and Redeemer and praying for victory over its enemies which are no less deadly because they are spiritual, subtle and unseen.

2   It is the prayer book of Christ himself. In his own use of them its words of adoration, supplication and self-committal were brought to their perfect end.

Using the Psalter in the name of Christ the members of the Body make their own the prayer of the Head.

May we never have a generation of worshippers unfamiliar with the Canticles and the Psalms!

The Liturgy of the Eucharist

The Eucharist is the supreme way in which the people of Christ are, through our Great High Priest, with God with the world around on their hearts.

The author and the agent in the Eucharist is the Word of God. The Word is proclaimed in the scripture lections and in the preaching. Then the same Word, who is Jesus, blesses the loaf and the cup, and invites and commands us.

Jesus the Word feeds us so that we may be increasingly his own Body in the world to share with him in his work of the world's re-creation. He does not feed us in order to draw us away with him into a separated realm of religion, but to draw us into participation with him in the work of moulding the world into his own likeness.

And the meaning of all life is here set forth, since men exist to worship God for God's own sake.

Like the incarnation itself, the Eucharist is the breaking into history of something eternal, beyond history, inapprehensible in terms of history alone.

The supreme question is not what we make of the Eucharist but what the Eucharist is making of us, as (together with the Word) it fashions us into the way of Christ.

God is the friend of man

God is the friend of man, and in any exchange between God and man, God will be the one who is giving far more, giving so much that what man gives seems feeble, tiny, almost nothing.

That is the meaning of Christmas, Good Friday and Easter — God giving himself in generous self-giving to mankind, so that he is near us, with us, in us in ways beyond our imagining.

God and us; yes, God and us together, and together in a wonderful nearness.

And when we pray we will not be bombarding God with our own desires. We will be starting far nearer to God, sharing a little of his heart and mind, and putting our will at his disposal to serve his good purpose to the world.

God's purpose

God's purpose is like a stream of goodness flowing out into the world and all its needs.

But it is our privilege as God's children to help this stream to reach other people, becoming ourselves like channels.

Our good actions can be channels of God's goodness, and so too can our prayers . . .

Isn't this what Jesus tells us when he gives us the 'Our Father' as our model prayer? Jesus meant not only 'pray in these words', but 'pray with this sequence of thought and desire'. . .

When we say that God loves us we mean that he cares for each single one of us as if there is no one else for him to care for; he cares for you in all that unique individuality which is yours. He wants *you*, to be with him, for ever, to share with you all he has to share.

That is heaven.

It is the perfection of the God and man relation. And it cannot be selfish in any way, because it implies the plural, and heaven includes the mutual love and service of all who share it together, a love and service totally integrated with the love of God and the vision of God.

Pilgrimage to Lindisfarne

In a few hours the tide will ebb, and we shall turn our steps back to our homes, back to our daily tasks, back again to our parishes and our churches . . . My children, carry back with you the supreme lesson of this holy island: carry it back.

The supreme lesson is that our fathers came here because they knew that, if souls were to be won, there comes first the call of prayer to God, in quiet, in separation from the whirl of the world's life. Carry this back.

Priests, put first of all your prayer: be men of God: be intercessors. Follow Cuthbert who 'when he offered the holy mysteries offered himself a sacrifice to God with tears of contrition'.

People, get quiet for your prayers: use your churches for quiet, silent prayer – and heaven will be a little nearer. Carry this back; it is the good part, the one thing needful which Mary chose.

The glory of us children is our fathers: remember them: thank God for them: imitate their faith. And the mighty purpose of God will move forward, and instead of our fathers there shall be our children, princes of Christ in our own and every land.

The prayer of simply being oneself

No one is nearer to God than the man who has a hunger, a want – however tiny and inarticulate.

And that is where prayer can begin, the prayer of simply being oneself in utter sincerity.

One can pray like this: 'O my God, I want thee, help me to want thee more.' 'O my God, I love thee so little, help me to love thee as thou lovest me.' 'O my God, I scarcely believe in thee, increase my tiny faith.' 'O my God, I do not really feel sorry for my sin: but I want to, give me a true sorrow for it.'

We don't find God by trying to be more religious than we are or can be.

No, we are near God by being true to ourselves, and then God can begin to find us, to fill our emptiness, and some of the old phrases of religion can be near to what is in the heart.

Intercession

Concerning intercession: the Church is called to be a community which speaks to the world in God's name and speaks to God from the middle of the world's darkness and frustration.

What is called the intercession of Jesus means his ceaseless presence with the Father. He is with the Father not as begging the Father to be gracious, for from the Father graciousness ever flows.

To approach the Father through Jesus Christ the intercessor is to approach in awareness of the cost of our redemption by a sacrifice made once for all and a victory once accomplished, a sacrifice and victory which are both past history and ever-present realities. It is this which both enables and characterizes our response to God through Jesus Christ.

To intercede is to bear others on the heart in God's presence. Our own wantings have their place, for it is clear from the teaching of Jesus that God wants us to want and to tell him of our wants. When, however, we do this 'in the name of Jesus' we learn to bend our wantings to our glimpses of the divine will. Intercession thus becomes not the bombardment of God with requests so much as the bringing of our desires within the stream of God's own compassion.

Silence

Silence enables us to be aware of God, to let mind and imagination dwell upon his truth, to let prayer be listening before it is talking, and to discover our own selves in a way that is not always possible when we are making or listening to noise. There comes sometimes an interior silence in which the soul discovers itself in a new dimension of energy and peace, a dimension which the restless life can miss.

A world frightening in its speed and noise is a world where silence alone may enable man's true freedom to be found.

A time of silence enables the Christian to share more deeply in the Church's sacramental worship. Into the Christian's use of silence there may flow the wonder of God the Creator, the recollection of the life and death and resurrection of Jesus, the recalling of scenes in his life, often a passage of the Bible, the glories of nature in which the finger of God is present, gratitude for personal blessings or the words of poets who tell of wonder and beauty.

Be still and know: the prayer of contemplation

There are signs of a recovery of the contemplative spirit with the realization that contemplation is an exposure to the divine love powerful in its effects upon a human life.

The effect of contemplation is often not to cause the person to long for experiences so much as to love and serve God under the sovereignty revealed in Jesus. Indeed, the validity of contemplation is often tested by the pursuit of the life of faith.

Christian prayer and Christian life are described both by St Paul and by St John as including a deep indwelling of God and of Jesus in the Christians, an anticipation of the glory of the parousia. We are not far from contemplation when we read, 'If a man love me he will keep my word, and my Father will love him and we will come and make our dwelling with him.'

It matters greatly for the renewal of the Christian Church that the contemplative vocation be more known and recovered. It matters for us all, whatever our own form of service, for we are all one family. Just as it helps us in our day-to-day struggles that there are martyrs who have given their lives for Christ, so it helps us in our feeble praying that there are those who know the Dark Night and have God himself poured into their souls.

Things that are not shaken: the religious life

Through the centuries, Christ has called some to the religious life in the threefold vows of poverty, chastity, obedience. Here is an intensely evangelical part of Christianity, rooted in the gospel story.

And as to the religious vows. These are not presumptuous. Rather the vows of religion mean the total acceptance of the call of God and the gift from God – an acceptance 'by faith alone' and 'by grace alone'. To God alone be the glory.

Now there was perhaps never a time when the religious life was more significant in Christendom and in the world than today. If God calls and if God disposes gifts, the call and the gifts are true and valid in their own right because they are God's; but yet we are able to see how God's call and God's gifts can answer the problems and needs of different epochs in history.

And as to the life of a religious community. Here its stability and its permanence has a telling, divine meaning.

It stands for the permanence of the vocation in its members, but it stands also for a witness to things that are not shaken, to truths and ideals which are not of any one age but reach across the centuries, a ladder set up and its top reaches to heaven.

Obedience

We are servants, called upon to obey.

Has not the idea of obedience as a Christian virtue rather slipped out of our contemporary religion? We think much about the responses of faith, love, sonship, friendship in our relation to God or to our Lord. But obedience? We tend to think that it smacks of legalism, and not to dwell upon it.

But it has an ineradicable place in the New Testament. Jesus was 'obedient unto death' (Philippians 2:8), and 'he learned obedience through what he suffered' (Hebrews 5:8).

The apostle is Christ's slave.

Our obedience calls for 'loins girded'.

'Loins girded' suggests an alertness which is ready to meet emergencies and interruptions. Do not be encumbered. Be ready to move, rapidly and unexpectedly. Our faithfulness is again and again tested by our power to deal with interruptions. You plan your day according to some rule, then all seems thrown into disorder by interruptions.

If the will of God is that you should accept this or that interruption, and you accept them with gladness, then a day which might seem tempestuous is really filled with plan and peace and order; for where the will of God is there is God's presence and God's peace, and where that will is obeyed there is pattern and harmony. In his will is your peace.

Joy

Joy in the Lord. What is this joy?

It is the joy experienced by those who, come what may, are beginning to know God, to enjoy God in his beauty and loveliness, and to be exposed to his energies.

It is not only the joy of a sure faith that God reigns supreme; it is the joy of a practical fellowship with one who is himself joy and pours joy into lives which are united with him.

Our joy is the joy of those who are forgiven and forgiving. Lose hold on the realities of penitence and forgiveness in your life, and it will not be surprising if the joy which is your privilege begins to fade.

To have joy in God means knowing that God is our country, our environment, the air we breathe. 'God is the country of the soul,' said St Augustine. Living in that country, we do not turn away from the griefs of our present environment – indeed, we may expect a greater sensitivity to these – but we are in the perspective of God, of heaven, of eternity.

Suffering and circumstance transfigured

The 'Our Father' takes the needs and the agonizing conflicts of mankind and lifts them into the realm of the Kingdom and the Father.

Transfiguration is indeed a central theme of Christianity, the transforming of sufferings and circumstances, of men and women with the vision of Christ before them and the Holy Spirit within them.

The transfiguring of suffering is attested in Christian life. Sometimes a person suffers greatly, and the suffering continues and does not disappear; but through nearness to Christ there is seen a courage, an outgoing love and sympathy, a power of prayer, a Christlikeness of a wonderful kind.

Circumstances are transfigured. Something blocks your path, some fact of life or person or obstacle which is utterly thwarting and frustrating. It seems impossible to remove it or ignore it or surmount it. But when it is seen in a larger context, and that context is Jesus crucified and risen, it is in a new orbit of relationships and while it remains, it remains differently. A phrase of St Paul seems to interpret the experience, when he contrasts our 'light affliction' with the 'exceeding weight of glory', the one belonging to time and the other to eternity. Such is the transforming of circumstances, not by their abolition but by the lifting of them into the orbit of a crucified and risen Jesus.

Holiness

The idea of *holiness* finds a new emphasis in the early Church. In the new covenant the role of the 'holy nation' is now taken over by the Christians; they are the *ecclesia* of God, they are called to be holy, they are the elect race, the holy nation, the people for God's possession (1 Peter 2:9).

The use of *hoi hagioi*, the holy ones, as the normal description of the Christians, brings out the new and overwhelming emphasis upon holiness in Christianity.

So life in the Spirit is holiness.

Possessing holiness in the call of God and in the Spirit of holiness, the Church grows along the way of Christ's holiness.

Unity, holiness, truth; as the prayer of our Great High Priest is indivisible, so the fulfilment is indivisible too. It is useless to think that we can look for unity in Christ's name unless we are looking no less for holiness in his obedience and for the realization of the truth which he has revealed.

All the while Christ the Head of the Church goes on in his mercy using the Church, divided though it be, to make known his truth and unity and to lead many in the way of saintliness.

The role of Christians in the world

We are called as Christians to a faith which both cares intensely about this world and is also set upon another world beyond it.

The first is an immediate test of our Christianity. Our concern in action for the hungry and the homeless, for right dealing between different races, for the laws of conduct which God has given us, shows whether we love God whom we have not seen by the test of our love for the brother we have seen.

But as we serve this world and its needs we are all the while laying hold of something beyond this world, an eternal life which gives this world its true perspective. Let that not be forgotten.

We are here not only to do things, we are here to be something, to become something – and that is the meaning of our being called to be saints. Christianity is about our doing things here, and about our being something whose goal is beyond here.

The Christians are in the world as the soul is in the body by keeping alive for themselves and for others the hope of heaven.

To this he has called us, and has made us one with all in every place who have the same call and dare not look back.

Openness to the world

Through lack of openness to the contemporary world theology has sometimes worked in a kind of vacuum with neither meaningfulness for itself nor power of self-communication.

Openness to the world must always be accompanied by an openness to Christ crucified, or else the world's wisdom can mislead.

The need is for every kind of openness – to the past and to the present, to the world and to heaven and eternity.

Thus our openness to heaven is null and void unless it carries with it an openness to the world around us. With the daily decisions and relationships of the world around us we encounter God, and we learn the meaning of our theology in human terms.

Those who would isolate the secular city from the past and from eternity lose the dimension in which human lives have their ultimate meaning and the perspective in which the needs of the secular city are rightly seen.

Nowhere more vividly than in the sacrament of the Eucharist do Christians find through Christ an openness to the past and to the present, to heaven and to the world.

Through this openness the Christian is equipped to face the tasks of the present with realism and to face the future with hope.

Whose hearts God has touched

All the time there is, for us whose hearts God has touched, the supreme task to bring home to the people of God himself, in his majesty, his compassion, his claim upon mankind, his astounding gift of his very self in Jesus the Word-made-Flesh.

We cannot fulfil the task for this country unless we are striving to fulfil it towards the whole of the world. It therefore demands the service of men and women who will go anywhere in the world in Christ's obedience, who will witness to Christ's love in the insistence that races, black and white, are brothers of equal worth.

Here at home our mission means for the Church a constant involvement in the community. We must approach as learners as well as teachers. We need to be learning not only many new techniques, but also what God is saying to us through the new and exciting circumstances of our time.

Because it is God to whom we witness, we need no less a constant detachment, a will to go apart and wait upon God in quiet, in silence, lest by our very busyness we should rob ourselves and rob others of the realization of God's presence: 'Be still and know that I am God.'

Would that everyone whose heart God has touched would guard times of quietness amid our noisy, bustling life, to let God touch the heart again.

Sources and index

The following editions have been used:

The Gospel and the Catholic Church (Longmans 1936); *The Glory of God and the Transfiguration of Christ* (Longmans 1949); *Durham Essays and Addresses* (SPCK 1936); *The Meaning of Prayer* (Mowbrays 1965); *Jesus, The Living Lord* (a lecture given at Canterbury Cathedral 2 November 1966 and privately printed); *God, Christ and the World* (SCM 1969); *Freedom, Faith and the Future* (SPCK 1970); *The Future of the Christian Church* (with Archbishop Suenens) (Morehouse-Barlow, New York 1970); *Canterbury Pilgrim* (SPCK 1974); *Holy Spirit* (SPCK 1977); *Lent with St John* (SPCK 1980); *Be Still and Know* (Collins Fount 1982); *Constantinople 381*. The Constantinople Lecture (Anglican and Eastern Churches Association 1982); *The Christian Priest Today* (new and revised edn, SPCK 1985).

The figures in bold type below refer to the pages of Readings in this book. They are followed by the Sources.

57 *Holy Spirit* 62, 63, 65, 88
   Canterbury Essays and Addresses 55, 59
58 *Canterbury Pilgrim* 97, 98
59 *God, Christ and the World* 114, 115, 116
60 *Canterbury Essays and Addresses* 167–8